A History of American Music

COUNTRY

Christopher Handyside

Heinemann Library
Chicago, Illinois

Customer Service   888–454–2279
Visit our website at www.heinemannraintree.com

Photo research by Hannah Taylor, Maria Joannou,
and Erica Newbery
Designed by Philippa Baile and Ron Kamen
Printed in China by WKT Company Limited

10 09 08 07 06
10 9 8 7 6 5 4 3 2 1

Library of Congress Cataloging-in-Publication Data
Handyside, Chris.
Country / Christopher Handyside.
p. cm. – (A history of American music)
Includes bibliographical references (p.   ) and
index.
ISBN 1-4034-8151-2 (hc)
1. Country music–History and criticism–Juvenile
literature. I. Title.
II. Series.
ML3524.H26 2006
781.642'0973–dc22   2005019281

Acknowledgments
The author and publishers are grateful to the
following for permission to reproduce copyright
material:
John Byrne Cooke Photos p. 4; Corbis p. 5;
Corbis/Bettmann pp. 6, 16, 17, 25, 35 top, 37;
Corbis/Reuters p. 41 top & bottom; Getty Images
pp. 30 (Agence France Presse), 13, 34 (Frank
Driggs Collection), 11, 24, 27 (Hulton Archive);
Redferns pp. 9, 22, 32 (GAB Archives), 14, 15 top,
18, 19, 20, 29, 31, 35 bottom, 43 (Michael Ochs
Archive), 21 (RB), 33 (David Redfern), 15 bottom
(Nicky J. Sims), 23; Topfoto pp. 7 (Roger-Viollet),
40 (Image Works); Topham
Picturepoint/Bandphoto/uppa.co.uk p. 39.

Cover photograph of a banjo player reproduced
with permission of Corbis (Paul A. Souders).

The publishers would like to thank Patrick Allen for
his assistance with the preparation of this book.

Words shown in **boldface** are defined in the
glossary on page 46.

Contents

Mountain Beginnings

Country is one of the United States' most enduring and evolving musical styles. Country music was born in the foothills of the Appalachian Mountain range in the 1800s. Immigrants from the British Isles brought their traditional folk songs with them when they settled in the United States. Until the widespread use of phonographs and records, these songs were largely an **oral tradition**. This means that they were passed from generation to generation. Each new generation of rural Americans adapted the songs and lyrics to their particular environment and lifestyle.

Like the **blues**, early country music was simple and straightforward. The lyrics were **nostalgic** stories, spiritual songs, and tales of hard times. The music was played mostly on the **fiddle** and the guitar, and later, the banjo. The players' isolated location played a part in forming the old-time country music style. However, there were also some outside influences. For example, in the 1880s, a musical group from Switzerland toured the South and introduced the people of the region to the vocal technique known as **yodeling**. This is when a singer suddenly changes his or her voice's pitch from its normal range to a high falsetto and back again. Yodeling became the trademark of many country singers in the years that followed.

The first strains of country music could be heard from the homes of second-generation Americans.

At the same time in the West, in places such as Texas and Oklahoma, cowboys developed a culture of sharing stories and songs around the campfire. These songs would later influence country music. They also gave birth to the name "Country and Western" and the myth of the "singing cowboy" in Hollywood movies.

In these ways, country was a type of "folk" music, played by non-professionals for their own entertainment. In the early 1900s, **folklorists** started collecting country and cowboy folk songs. They first did this in the form of written songbooks, and later in early, crude recordings. As the recording business developed, companies like Decca and Vocalion, from New York City and Chicago, sent talent scouts to areas around the South and West to look for new talent. These songbooks and recordings, as well as the possibility of making records, kick started the popularity of country music. Musicians began to come out of the hills and prairies to perform their music professionally.

In the West, cowboys shared songs to kill the long hours while they drove cattle across long distances.

Early Country

In 1922, the Victor Company made the first recordings of what is known as "hillbilly music." A "big city" **field recorder**, or folklorist, recorded a fiddler named Eck Robertson, and others like him. Some of these folklorists were eager to sell their recordings to other people living in the country. This was still music that was regional in its appeal. This means that it didn't really sell outside the area where the recording artist was popular. Because these artists often lived in the regions around mountain ranges, like the Smokey Mountains or the Blue Ridge Mountains, they were called "hillbillies." The name hillbilly stuck when people were asked to describe the kind of music they made. The term "country" music wasn't used until the late 1940s.

Country folk in the 1920s dancing to the music of banjos and fiddle in front of a farmhouse in Virginia.

By the 1920s, the phonograph, an early form of gramophone, was starting to become commercially available. Previously, the music of popular bands and musicians was spread to the fans by sheet music and songbooks. Now, albums—specifically 78 rpm records—were starting to make a commercial impact.

In the South, blues and jazz recordings were sold to largely black audiences. The early blues records were called "**race records**" when marketed to white audiences. This was a whole new market. The white version of bluesy race records was hillbilly music. Hillbilly and race records would usually be found next to each other in record stores.

Invented in 1877 by Thomas Edison, the phonograph was the earliest player of recorded music. In the very early days, recordings were made on rotating cylinders of tinfoil or wax, which the phonograph needle could read.

Later, records made from shellac and vinyl became the most popular medium for recorded music, until the invention of casette tapes and CDs. Records were designated by their speed—78, 45, or 33 rpm. The letters "rpm" stand for revolutions per minute, or the speed at which the record spins. Many of the early country, blues, and jazz recordings were made for 78 rpm.

This late 1920s wind-up gramophone was an improvement on the early phonographs.

One of the earliest stars of hillbilly music was Uncle Dave Macon. In the 1910s and 1920s, Macon traveled around the Nashville area selling the crops grown at his family's farm in nearby Murfreesboro, Tennessee. He would pull into a town and perform traditional mountain songs and ballads on his banjo to attract customers to his wagon. By the 1920s, trucks had taken over from the horse-drawn wagon, and Macon had to work even harder to attract a crowd.

In 1924, a talent scout spotted him singing and signed him to a contract as a musician. Macon recorded a number of songs for the Vocalion label in the mid-1920s and became a popular regional entertainer. He also became an important part of the *Grand Ole' Opry*, a popular country music radio show of the late 1920s. He performed regularly on the show for nearly 30 years until his death in 1952, at the age of 82. Uncle Dave Macon was one of country music's first real stars, as well as a vital connection to country music's hillbilly and folk past.

Another well-known, early hillbilly performer of the era was singer Vernon Dalhart. Dalhart's ballad, "Wreck of the Old '97," was the first hillbilly recording to be a big seller outside of the South. Other important performers from this era include fiddler Eck Robertson, Dock Boggs, and Fiddlin' John Carson. All of these artists provided a musical and cultural link to the music passed down from family member to family member in mountain communities since the 1800s.

After spending the first 50 years of his life as a farmer, Uncle Dave Macon turned his music hobby into a career.

The First Family of Country

Ralph Peer was a traveling talent scout for Victor Records in New York City. In August 1927, on one of his frequent trips to the South, he drove into Bristol, Tennessee.

Peer had already won acclaim as the man who recorded the first black blues song in 1920—Mamie Smith's "Crazy Blues." In 1923 he had also made the first commercial recordings of country musicians, including Atlanta mill worker Fiddlin' John Carson's "The Little Old Log Cabin in the Lane." Peer had come upon quite a few remarkable musical finds in these rural towns.

Peer set up a temporary recording studio in an abandoned factory and began recording. The country folk lined up to audition for him. Little did he know that by the end of the session, he would have encountered some of the most important artists in the history of country music.

Before Peer was done, the recordings that eventually started the country music industry were in his trunk. When A.P., Sara, and Maybelle Carter, also known as the Carter Family, came to his studio that day, they performed a handful of songs that had been handed down through their family for generations. One thing that caught Peer's attention was guitarist Maybelle's unique form of playing. Maybelle would pick the melody on the lower strings of her guitar while simultaneously strumming the rhythm on the higher strings. This "Carter Style" would have a tremendous influence on future country guitar playing.

Alvin P. Carter (A.P.) with his wife Sara (right) and sister Maybelle formed the Carter Family trio.

The other discovery from Peer's trip was a blues-influenced guitar player and singer from Mississippi named Jimmie Rodgers. The former railroad brakeman had been playing in a band, but on the night of their tryout for Peer, Rodgers and his band mates got into an argument. The rest of the band went home, and Rodgers auditioned alone. His audition was good enough to land him a shot at recording for Victor Records.

Rodgers' first recording was the song that defined his career. It was a blues-based song called "Blue Yodel" that featured his distinctive yodeling technique. It sold more than a million copies and led to other hits for the so-called "Singing Brakeman." Rodgers was extremely successful regionally and nationally. Sadly, in 1933 he died of tuberculosis, a disease of the lungs that was common in the early part of the 1900s. Rodgers was only 35 when he passed away.

At the end of the 1920s, there was a stock market crash which triggered the **Great Depression**. This led to a decline in record sales. Radio's popularity was on the rise, however, and country music found a new home on national and international radio shows. Music by bands such as the Carter Family now reached a large audience, many of whom knew nothing about the rural mountain experience. But songs such as "Will the Circle Be Unbroken?" and "No Depression" were universal and timely enough to offer comfort and strength to listeners, no matter where they were from.

One of the most popular of these radio shows was the *WSM Barn Dance* out of Nashville. This showcased the best hillbilly artists. It would become a Nashville institution. Other shows, such as WLS radio's *National Barn Dance* out of Chicago and the *Louisiana Hayride*, were also popular. These shows had massive audiences. A good performance on one of these shows could make an artist's career. In 1928, the *WSM Barn Dance* was renamed the *Grand Ole' Opry*. The *Opry* eclipsed the other shows in popularity and secured its place in country legend.

Jimmy Rodgers' love of entertaining came early. By age 13, he had twice run off with traveling shows, and had to be brought back home by his father.

The Singing Brakeman

13

We'll Go Honky Tonkin'

During the 1940s, country music was often performed in rough bars called "honky-tonks" throughout the South—especially in Texas—where rural white people would go to dance and listen to music. Over the years, honky-tonk became the term to describe a style of blues piano playing, as well as this early style of raw, simple country music. Acoustic guitar and fiddle were the primary lead instruments. Stand-up or string bass added **rhythm**. The singers sang in a nasal, twangy style that exaggerated their southern accents, and often featured vocal stutters, or "hiccups." Songs were about heartbreak, good times, and bad times. In short, honky-tonk was tales of everyday life set to music you could dance to. Many people first think of honky-tonk music when they think of country. Now, "country" describes a much wider variety of music.

Early honky-tonk stars included Ernest Tubb, Lefty Frizzell, and Hank Williams. Of these, the first to really become a star was Tubb, who had hits with 1943's "Walkin' the Floor With You," as well as later favorites, such as "Let's Say Goodbye Like We Said Hello" and "Have You Ever Been Lonely (Have You Ever Been Blue)?"

Ernest Tubb (center) on stage with the Texas Troubadors.

Wild country boy, Hank Williams Sr.

The truly legendary figure to emerge from the early honky-tonk years was Hank Williams. In 1947, Williams became hugely popular with songs such as "Honky Tonkin'" and the rollicking "Move It On Over," as well as his live shows. Unfortunately, he was almost as well known for his reckless behavior as for his music. On New Year's Eve 1953, Williams died in the back seat of his Cadillac on the way to a show in Ohio. His last hit record had been "I'll Never Get Out of This World Alive."

Williams' musical legacy lit a fire under country music that hasn't been extinguished yet. Through the years, singers such as George Jones in the 1950s and 1960s, and modern stars like Alan Jackson and Randy Travis, kept the honky-tonk spirit alive in their music. Later, the Hank Williams style was to have a major influence on early, white rock 'n' roll artists such as Elvis Presley, Carl Perkins, and Jerry Lee Lewis.

Hank Williams III.

Hank Williams' legacy didn't live on solely through his music. His oldest son, Hank Jr., made a name for himself starting in the 1950s and 1960s. During this time, Hank Jr. imitated his father's honky-tonk style. But in mid-1970s, after a long recovery from a horrific fall off a mountain, Hank Jr. started afresh. His first release after his fall came in 1975. "The New South" was right in line with the raucous, rock 'n' roll-influenced style of music called "outlaw country." Hank Jr. began making a new name for himself with more rock-based songs such as "All My Rowdy Friends (Have Settled Down)" and "Born To Boogie." By the end of the 1980s, he stopped charting new songs, but he still remains a popular live performer. Hank Jr. found his way onto national television in the 1990s as the voice and face of the Monday Night Football theme "Are You Ready For Some Football?" on ABC television.

The rebel legacy continued with Hank Jr.'s son Hank Williams III. Hank III also got his start as "the grandson of Hank Williams," but he soon followed his true musical passion, which was a hard, fast, **punk-rock** version of "country." Hank III's maverick attitude and rough 'n' ready music was first heard on his 1999 album, *Risin' Outlaw.*

Lonesome Cowboy

During the 1930s and 1940s, country music became even more popular through Hollywood's "singing cowboy" movies. There were, of course, real singing cowboys. In 1910, folklorist John Lomax released a book of songs he had collected while traveling the West, titled *Cowboy Songs and Other Frontier Ballads*. These were songs sung around the campfire by non-professional singers. The notion of the singing cowboy became popular in the 1930s, with the movies of country musician-turned-actor Gene Autry. Autry grew up in Texas and began singing in his grandfather's church. After traveling in **medicine shows**, he became a star on WLS radio's *National Barn Dance* out of Chicago. His movies were usually romantic Westerns shot on the wide-open plains with a few songs performed by the cowboy hero. The songs "Home on the Range" and "Tumbling Tumbleweeds" date from this period of movie-making. Besides Autry, Roy Rogers and Tex Ritter were perhaps the most famous singing cowboys.

The idea that these movies could make a profit began with the popularity of Texas groups such as Milton Brown and his Musical Brownies, and especially Bob Wills and his Texas Playboys. These bands mostly played at dance halls throughout Texas and Oklahoma. The music they played suited the rowdiness of the dancing scene. It was a mix of traditional country fiddle songs and the big-band swing blues music that was all the rage in New York City. This music was called "Western Swing."

"Singing cowboy" Gene Autry was also one of the greatest trick horse riders in motion picture history.

Western Swing highlighted Bob Wills' **virtuosity** on his instrument and his yodeling singing voice. Ironically, Wills did not know how to read or write music. Instead, he played entirely by ear. He could imitate any song played for him. His band was wildly successful, and released many hit records. In Texas and Oklahoma, Wills was the undisputed "King of Western Swing."

By the mid-1930s, a large number of Oklahomans (or "Okies," as they were called) and Texans had moved to Southern California to escape the **Dust Bowl** and find new work. These transplanted Southerners brought with them their love of country music, particularly the Western Swing of Bob Wills. By the time the music took hold among Californians, bandleader Spade Cooley had been crowned the new "King of Western Swing" (by his own promoter). These bands stayed popular for a few years until the United States entered World War II in 1941.

In many ways, World War II brought Americans together in ways they had not experienced before. **G.I.**s from the South learned about the culture of the North, and vice versa. This kind of cultural exchange, plus the increasing availability of country records, helped country music to gain even greater national popularity. After 1941, country music became a fully-fledged industry based in Nashville, Tennessee.

Cowboy bandleader Bob Wills with his vocalist and guitarist Tommy Duncan (right) in 1944.

Bluegrass Kicks Up Its Heels

Though **bluegrass** seems like music as old as the hills, it is actually a relatively recent development. It was brought to the public's attention in 1939 by band leader Bill Monroe, whose band the Blue Grass Boys recorded "Mule Skinner Blues."

Bill Monroe on vocals with his Blue Grass Boys.

People responded to the irresistible energy and rhythm of bluegrass, plucked out on the banjo and buffered by guitar, **mandolin**, and fiddle. Monroe's high singing voice seemed to come straight out of the Smokey Mountains, with its yodeling, hiccupy characteristics. Bluegrass was popular from the beginning because it represented a homegrown music from the hills of Tennessee, North Carolina, and Kentucky. During the 1940s, it was seen as a genuine alternative to the growing slickness of the country music emerging from Nashville.

Two of Monroe's former band members did more than anyone to make bluegrass popular. Guitar player and singer Lester Flatt and banjo picker extraordinaire Earl Scruggs joined Monroe's band in 1945 and soon began attracting attention for their fine playing. By 1948, they were confident enough in their abilities to leave Monroe and form their own band, The Foggy Mountain Boys. An angry Monroe had them **blacklisted** from the *Grand Ole' Opry* radio show. But despite this rocky start, Flatt and Scruggs signed a recording deal with Columbia records in 1950. The band flourished in the 1950s with a string of hit singles. Their popularity continued to grow as they recorded the theme songs to two popular television shows of the mid-1960s, "The Ballad of Jed Clampett" (for *The Beverly Hillbillies*) and "Petticoat Junction" (for the show of the same name). In 1969, their popular hit "Foggy Mountain Breakdown" was used in the soundtrack to Arthur Penn's film *Bonnie and Clyde*.

During the 1940s and 1950s, bluegrass continued to evolve in the work of such innovative players, singers, and songwriters as the great Ralph and Carter Stanley and their band, the Clinch Mountain Boys. The Stanleys made their first record in 1947. They helped to make bluegrass not just Bill Monroe's music, but a **bona fide** genre. The Stanleys' songs had a strong gospel element, especially when sung in the deep, powerful voice of Ralph Stanley.

In the 1960s, Del McCoury and his band carried on Monroe's brand of bluegrass. Mainstream popular interest in bluegrass waned, but it continued to have a loyal audience in the South, and among transplanted Southerners in Ohio, Illinois, and Michigan.

Bluegrass lives on today in the music of traditional players such as Allison Krauss and her band, Union Station. Master banjo player Bela Fleck and his Flecktones perform bluegrass with an experimental bent, mixing elements of rock and jazz. And in 2000, the soundtrack to the film *O, Brother, Where Art Thou?* renewed an interest in bluegrass music.

The astonishing virtuosity and talent of The Foggy Mountain Boys band helped to put bluegrass on the musical map.

The Seeds of The Nashville Sound

The beginning of country music's mainstream popularity can be directly linked to the rise of the city of Nashville, Tennessee as the center of the country music industry. By the early 1940s, Nashville was already a destination for many traveling musicians from around the South, thanks to its central location in the region and the popularity and prestige of the *Grand Ole' Opry*. Artists such as Roy Acuff and Ernest Tubb had made Nashville their home. Their popularity led many country musicians and songwriters to head for Nashville, hoping to be discovered.

The turning point for Nashville's fame came when Acuff and his business partner Fred Rose founded the very first country music publishing business in the city. They called this company Acuff-Rose. A music publisher is responsible for purchasing the works of songwriters and convincing artists to record the songs. Acuff-Rose published virtually all of the songs that were written by Nashville-based songwriters. They then represented them to record industry executives from New York, Los Angeles, and other cities.

Acuff-Rose gave the homegrown Nashville artists bargaining power with these big city labels. Hundreds of aspiring musicians and songwriters headed to Nashville to try to score a hit with Acuff-Rose. Because they needed somewhere to record, a booming studio business grew up in Nashville, too. By 1944, the music had its own popularity chart in *Billboard Magazine*, the bible of the commercial music business. The magazine called this chart the "country" chart.

Roy Acuff was a minor-league baseball player before an injury ended his career. After this disappointment, he learned to play his father's fiddle.

Country music fans in the 1950s, lining up outside The Grand Ole' Opry House in Nashville.

The growth of the various businesses that supported the homegrown music industry became known as Nashville's "Music Row"—a district of town where studios, labels, and other related businesses are centered.

By the late 1940s and early 1950s, Nashville had produced hits for honky-tonk stars Hank Williams, Lefty Frizzell, and Faron Young. In the late 1940s, a singer named Muriel Deason changed her name to Kitty Wells and became the "Queen of Country Music." Her solo career began in 1952 with the hit record "It Wasn't God Who Made Honky Tonk Angels." In the 1960s she recorded other hits, such as "Lonely Side of Town." Wells was a direct inspiration for many female Nashville singers, such as Loretta Lynn and the legendary Patsy Cline.

Rockabilly

A famous photo of the so-called Million Dollar Quartet at Sun Studio. From left to right, Jerry Lee Lewis, Carl Perkins, Elvis Presley (seated) and Johnny Cash.

In the early 1950s, country music was making waves in the popular charts among white listeners. Meanwhile, black musicians had been popularizing a mix of up-tempo blues music called rhythm & blues (R&B) in roadhouses across the South. It was the kind of music that people could dance to. Singers such as Arthur "Big Boy"Crudup became popular with songs like "That's All Right." Jackie Brenston and his Delta Cats blended jazz's boogie-woogie piano style with a rollicking blues tempo on their 1951 hit, "Rocket 88." This was one of rock 'n' roll's earliest records. It influenced the country artists who developed the new form of music called "rockabilly." Rockabilly was the product of white musicians playing in the style of the black R&B musicians they were hearing.

In 1954, a young country boy from Tupelo, Mississippi named Elvis Presley walked into Memphis producer Sam Phillips' Sun Records studio. He wanted to record a version of Crudup's "That's All Right" as a birthday gift for his mother. Elvis not only went on to become known as "The King" of rock 'n' roll, but his recordings inspired many other kids to record their own take on the country/R&B **hybrid**.

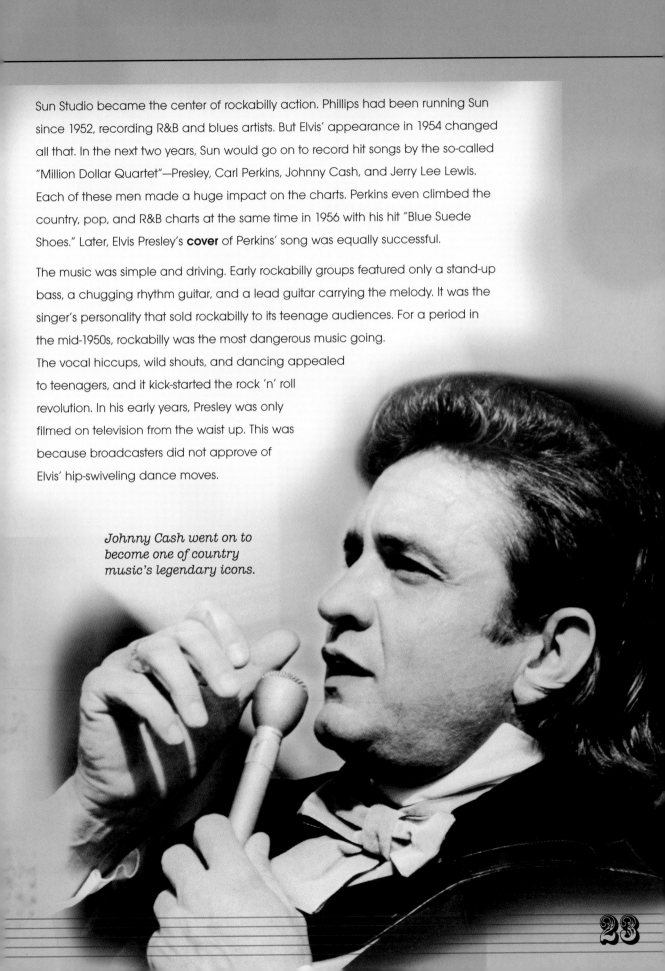

Sun Studio became the center of rockabilly action. Phillips had been running Sun since 1952, recording R&B and blues artists. But Elvis' appearance in 1954 changed all that. In the next two years, Sun would go on to record hit songs by the so-called "Million Dollar Quartet"—Presley, Carl Perkins, Johnny Cash, and Jerry Lee Lewis. Each of these men made a huge impact on the charts. Perkins even climbed the country, pop, and R&B charts at the same time in 1956 with his hit "Blue Suede Shoes." Later, Elvis Presley's **cover** of Perkins' song was equally successful.

The music was simple and driving. Early rockabilly groups featured only a stand-up bass, a chugging rhythm guitar, and a lead guitar carrying the melody. It was the singer's personality that sold rockabilly to its teenage audiences. For a period in the mid-1950s, rockabilly was the most dangerous music going. The vocal hiccups, wild shouts, and dancing appealed to teenagers, and it kick-started the rock 'n' roll revolution. In his early years, Presley was only filmed on television from the waist up. This was because broadcasters did not approve of Elvis' hip-swiveling dance moves.

Johnny Cash went on to become one of country music's legendary icons.

Rockabilly was as much characterized by the rebellious spirit of its performers as its music. To 1950s audiences, piano player Jerry Lee Lewis was a shocking figure with his mane of wild, curly blond hair. He often played the piano in concert by stomping his foot on the keyboard, even going so far as to set the piano on fire from time to time. Virginia native Gene Vincent was another rockabilly rebel, with his black motorcycle leather, rebellious stance, and trademark, lip-curled sneer. In the 1950s, throughout the South, artists such as Billy Lee Riley, Johnny Burnette, and Wanda Jackson straddled the line between country and rock to enjoy record sales and long-lasting musical careers.

Artists like bespectacled Texan Buddy Holly took rockabilly in a pop direction with his sweet, catchy songs like "Peggy Sue" and "Rave On." However, just as Holly was reaching his popular peak in 1959, he died in a tragic plane crash near Clear Lake, Iowa with two other early rock 'n' roll stars, The Big Bopper and Richie Valens. By the 1960s, rockabilly became yesterday's news as the Beatles and the rest of the "British Invasion" hit American shores.

Buddy Holly in 1955.

Johnny Cash: The Man in Black

Johnny Cash opened his performance in Folsom Penitentiary with his hit song "Folsom Prison Blues." He was made an honorary life-termer by the inmates!

Perhaps no country artist commands as much respect as Johnny Cash. Cash was born February 26, 1932 in Kingsland, Arkansas. He started performing an aggressive strain of hillbilly music at an early age, and in 1954 found himself in Memphis, Tennessee, auditioning for Sam Phillips of Sun Records. His first hit came with the chugging and tough **devotional** song "I Walk the Line." Cash made his debut at the *Grand Ole' Opry* in 1957 wearing all black clothing. From that point forward, he was referred to as "The Man in Black."

In 1968, Cash married Maybelle Carter's daughter, June. The two had a tempestuous courtship that resulted in his recording her song "Ring of Fire."

He managed to balance both his rebellious and religious sides with a series of concerts performed at federal prisons during the 1960s. The most famous of these was his concert at California's maximum security Folsom Penitentiary, released as a live album in 1968. The rowdy reception Cash received at the prison proved that his music connected with even the most hardened hearts.

Cash's career spanned country, gospel music, spoken word, and a variety show on network television, which he hosted from 1969 to 1971. Toward the end of his life, he started gaining renewed critical and popular attention with his *American Recordings*. This album featured Cash, accompanied only by his **acoustic** guitar, covering songs by other artists such as Bruce Springsteen and Nine Inch Nails.

The album gave Cash a new audience of rock 'n' roll fans who would probably have never thought to give his music a chance. Johnny Cash died on September 12, 2003, and with him died a vital connection to the United States' musical past.

Prime Time for Country

Even though rockabilly's popularity only lasted about five years, its impact, especially on country music, was huge. It occurred at the chronological crossroads between old-style country, rhythm & blues, and the birth of rock 'n' roll, in the early 1950s. Country music had to grow up to survive. It lost its hillbilly edge, with the nasal vocals and the instruments associated with rural country, like the fiddle and banjo. From the late 1950s, many country records that came out of Nashville featured background choirs, lush string arrangements, and other sounds common to pop music records of the time. In the 1960s the Nashville Sound became a twangier, folksy version of the smooth pop that was topping the charts.

It was not just the sound that made Nashville. The business end of Nashville was now well established, too. Major labels Columbia and RCA established recording complexes on Music Row. Each label employed its own songwriters, producers, session men, and performers. Of these, the producer became the most important player in the Nashville system of making records. He would pick which artist would record which songs from which publishing house, which session men would play on them, how they were to be performed, and the overall "sound" of the record.

Publishing houses provided a never-ending supply of new songs for the producers to choose from. Houses like Acuff-Rose and Sure-Fire flourished under the pop-oriented Nashville Sound. Future stars like Willie Nelson and Roger Miller got their start as songwriters at this time. Nelson, for his part, scored an early hit when his song "Crazy" topped the country charts in 1961 for singer Patsy Cline.

The 1960s brought to the country and pop music charts such artists as Loretta Lynn, whose honest female perspective on life's troubles made her an unlikely icon with songs like the autobiographical "Coal Miner's Daughter." The highly produced Nashville style of the time also benefited the songwriting and performances of Porter Wagoner and the hard-living George Jones.

Loretta Lynn performing at the Grand Ole' Opry in the 1960s. Other prominent female country acts of the 1960s included Patsy Kline, Tammy Wynette and Skeeter Davis.

Female singers played an important role in popularizing the Nashville Sound in the 1950s and 1960s. Starting with Kitty Wells, known as the "Queen of Country," women singers would often record heartfelt replies to their male counterparts' songs of cheating women and hard times.

Loretta Lynn was born in 1935 in Butcher Holler, a mining community in the hills of Kentucky. Married at age 14, Lynn already had four children by the time she began singing seriously in 1961. After her first success with "I'm a Honky Tonk Girl" (a nod to the influence of Kitty Wells), she went on to write and record a string of hits through the 1960s and 1970s. At the same time as raising her kids, she was singing songs about such issues as birth control, divorce, and the women's movement.

Lynn's status as one of the greatest American country music icons endures. In 1976, the title of her most famous song "Coal Miner's Daughter" was borrowed for her bestselling autobiography, and in 1980 for an Oscar-winning film of her life, starring Sissy Spacek and Tommy Lee Jones. Lynn's latest album, *Van Lear Rose*, was produced in 2004 by Jack White of White Stripes.

This rise in the country industry resulted in two institutions that signaled country music was here to stay. The first was the Country Music Association's (CMA's) Country Music Hall Of Fame, which, in 1961, inducted Fred Rose, Hank Williams, and Jimmie Rodgers. Six years later, in 1967, the CMA held its first annual Country Music Awards show. By this time, many country songs were becoming **crossover** pop hits on a regular basis. Songs from 1967, like Glen Campbell's "Wichita Lineman" and Bobbie Gentry's "Ode to Billie Joe," used the language of country to tell their stories, but the elaborate instrumentation and slick production were 100 percent pop.

The hillbilly, banjo-picking side of country was not entirely forgotten. In 1969, CBS debuted the long-running television variety show *HeeHaw*, which both celebrated and made fun of hillbilly culture with its exaggerated backcountry stereotypes. Hosts Buck Owens and Roy Clark, both accomplished players with deep roots in country, traded barbs and jokes between performances by such Nashville heavyweights as Faron Young and George Jones.

In the 1960s a string of female country singers became hugely popular. One of these was Patsy Cline. Cline had a rich and dramatic, yet straightforward voice that helped her songs "I Fall To Pieces," "Crazy," and "Walkin' After Midnight" to become big hits. Tragically, in 1963 Cline died in a plane crash near Camden, Tennessee, on the way back home from a show.

Long before country icon Dolly Parton became a world-famous singer, songwriter, actress, and **entrepreneur**, she got her start writing and performing with singer-songwriter Porter Wagoner. In the late 1960s, she set out on her own, with songs including "I Will Always Love You" (famously covered by R&B singer Whitney Houston) and the haunting ballad "Jolene."

Tammy Wynette was another icon of 1960s Nashville, with a string of hits that started in 1968 with her signature song of womanly devotion "Stand By Your Man." This song had an added depth since at the time Wynette was married to fellow country star George Jones. Their marriage was a rocky one—which gave "Stand By Your Man" increased impact.

Tammy Wynette and George Jones'
marriage lasted only five years.
However they continued to record
together through to the mid-1990s.

Country Rock

In the 1960s, Nashville was a music world of its own, with its own sounds, songs, and ways of working. However, the roots of country music had an impact on the growing **countercultural** rock 'n' roll scene. A new generation of rock 'n' rollers began to incorporate American folk and country music into their style. Like many of the important moments in mid-1960s music, country rock started with Bob Dylan.

In 1966, Dylan was laid up for several months after a motorcycle accident. When he was able to get up and play again, he rented a house near Woodstock, New York, and recruited a band called the Hawks. The Hawks were the former backing band of rockabilly singer Ronnie Hawkins. The house became known as "Big Pink," and Dylan and the Hawks recorded hundreds of songs there over several months. These songs were a wide variety of styles from folk to rock, and from country to blues.

Bob Dylan learned to play the guitar and harmonica as a child.

Dylan had been exploring the roots and branches of country music. His first post-accident recording in 1967 was the album *John Wesley Harding*. This featured country-influenced songs and simple arrangements. His next record, *Nashville Skyline*, was even more influenced by country music. It was recorded with Nashville session musicians and kicked off with a duet between Dylan and country music icon Johnny Cash. Between 1966 and *Nashville Skyline*'s release in 1969, country rock had become a popular genre, with artists, such as the Byrds and the Grateful Dead, rediscovering the folk roots of country.

The most popular of these bands was the Byrds. Led by songwriters and guitarists Roger McGuinn and Gene Clark, the Byrds started playing Los Angeles coffeehouses. Their style mixed folk, rock 'n' roll, and country. Each of the band's members (including former mandolin player Chris Hillman) was well versed in country folk music. This influence was very obvious on the 1968 record *Sweetheart of the Rodeo*—widely regarded as the definitive country rock record.

The songwriter most responsible for the Byrds' embrace of country was Gram Parsons, who joined the Byrds shortly before the recording of *Sweetheart*. Florida native Parsons started experimenting in his teens with combining country music and rock 'n' roll. While at Harvard University in 1966, Parsons formed The Like, later renamed The International Submarine Band. He left college after just one semester and headed west, meeting Chris Hillman of the Byrds. Parsons joined the Byrds in time to help them record *Sweetheart*. He quit shortly after and took Chris Hillman with him to form the even more country-tinged Flying Burrito Brothers. Their album, *The Gilded Palace of Sin*, continued Parsons' musical development.

Gram Parsons was born into a family of wealthy fruit growers. He later attended Harvard University, but never graduated.

In his brief career, Parsons managed to spread the influence of country music through the top names in rock 'n' roll. He went solo in 1970 and began hanging out with the British rock band the Rolling Stones. Parsons' country influence on the band can be heard on the Rolling Stones' 1972 album *Exile on Main Street,* as well as other albums from that period.

Parsons also recorded two classic solo albums, *GP* in 1973 and *Grievous Angel* in 1974. He had recruited a backing band called the Fallen Angels that included singer Emmylou Harris. Harris would go on to have a career as one of the most artistically and commercially successful, country-influenced, female singer-songwriters of the 1970s. But Parsons wouldn't be around to see it happen. In September 1973 he died from a drug overdose. *Grievous Angel* was released after his death. With his two final albums he left behind several touchstones of country rock, including such moving compositions as "Love Hurts," "Brass Buttons," and "Hickory Wind."

Emmylou Harris continues to play country music and still wins awards for her country albums.

Take me home, country roads

Country rock truly crossed over to the mainstream in the 1970s when artists like the Eagles, Emmylou Harris, and Linda Ronstadt became massively popular. However, with the exception of Harris, less and less of the initial influence of country music could be heard as these acts' careers progressed, and they developed more of a "soft rock" sound.

Linda Ronstadt performing in 1976.

As a musician, actor, environmentalist, and humanitarian, the crossover country–folk artist John Denver held a unique position in the American music scene.

Born Henry John Deutschendorf in Roswell, New Mexico in 1943, he later changed his name to Denver as a tribute to his beloved Colorado where he lived for most of his adult life. At age 12 Denver took up learning acoustic guitar, and in 1964 joined the folksy Chad Mitchell Trio as lead singer. The group's popularity had begun to fade, but Denver's remarkable talents as a singer and songwriter helped to resuscitate their fortunes and they were signed by the Mercury label.

In 1969, Denver left the band to start off on a solo career. The next decade established him as one of the most popular recording artists of the 1970s. His easy melodies, masterful guitar technique, and distinctive singing voice gained him an enormous following of fans. Hits such as "Take Me Home, Country Roads," "Leaving on a Jet Plane," and "Rocky Mountain High," as well as albums like *An Evening With John Denver* and *Windsong*, achieved record sales figures worldwide.

A passionate environmentalist and humanitarian, Denver used his fame and his music to communicate his concerns for wildlife conservation and world poverty. At the height of his success in 1976, he co-founded the Windstar Foundation, an environmental education and research center. In the early 1980s, Denver's popularity as a performer began to fade but he continued to champion conservation and humanitarian projects around the world.

Another of Denver's great passions was flying, and he was an experienced pilot. But in October 1997, tragedy struck when his new, experimental, fibreglass airplane crashed off the coast of Monterey, CA, killing him instantly.

Outlaw Country

By the early 1970s, Nashville had dominated the country world for 25 years. The Nashville system was very strict. Singers, songwriters, and session musicians only recorded for certain labels. Also, the rebellious attitude of rock 'n' roll was really making its mark on up-and-coming country artists.

In 1970, singer-songwriter Willie Nelson was the first major artist to leave Nashville. He moved back home to a ranch outside Austin, Texas. Nelson had already had a successful career in Nashville for more than 15 years, writing classic country songs, including Patsy Cline's 1961 hit "Crazy" and Faron Young's chart-topping version of "Hello Walls." But by 1970, RCA records was having little success selling him as a recording artist, and Nelson was frustrated at the lack of creative control he had over his own records.

Nelson emerged in 1975 with what is regarded as one of the first "Outlaw Country" records, *Red Headed Stranger*. This music genre was referred to as Outlaw Country partly because the artists were not following Nashville's style. It also took its name from a

Willie Nelson in 1979.

1972 song recorded by Nelson's pal, Waylon Jennings, "Ladies Love Outlaws." In short, it meant that these musicians were hard-living, straight-talking Southerners who loved country music and a little rock 'n' roll rebellion. They were influenced by the 1960s and 1970s rock 'n' roll style called Southern Rock. This featured loud but intricate guitar playing that was heavily influenced by country picking. Lynyrd Skynyrd and the Allman Brothers were among this style's best-known bands.

Besides Nelson and Jennings, the Outlaws were also associated with musicians Bobby Bare, Kris Kristofferson, and David Allan Coe. Coe was perhaps the most outlandish. He wore rhinestone-studded leather jackets, biker caps, garish belt-buckles, and large earrings. Although he was a controversial figure, Coe's music was firmly grounded in traditional country. He wrote Johnny Paycheck's million-selling hit "Take This Job And Shove It."

The influence of the Outlaws lives on today, in the music of acclaimed singer-songwriters such as Ray Wylie Hubbard and Steve Earle. The Outlaw style has also influenced musicians like rapper/rocker artist Kid Rock, who fancies himself a country boy at heart and has even played shows with David Allan Coe.

Waylon Jennings was a guitarist with Buddy Holly's touring band before Holly's death in 1959.

David Allan Coe, the self-styled "Mysterious Rhinestone Cowboy."

The New Nashville

By the mid-1970s, the country music coming out of Nashville had very little to do with the original country music of just two decades earlier. The Nashville Sound, with its factory-like efficiency and highly polished recordings, came to its peak in the late 1970s and 1980s. Country music's producers had become so good at creating records that were meant to appeal to a popular audience that the music they made during this time was indistinguishable from mainstream pop and rock acts. Gone was the sense of grit that had found its way through even the most popular country songs of the 1960s.

The new, slick country included an acceptance of rock 'n' roll style and Las Vegas glitz. A Texas singer named Kenny Rogers understood the formula early. He broke from his Nashville-based vocal group, the First Edition, in 1975. By the late 1970s, Rogers had become a very successful solo artist. His hits included "Lucille," "Coward of the County," and "The Gambler."

During the 1980s, Rogers also tried his hand at acting—with some success. His 1982 movie, *Six Pack*, grossed over $20 million at the U.S. box office. In it, Rogers plays a race-car driver whose car is stolen by six orphan kids and who ends up becoming their reluctant father-figure. Rogers also made several made-for-TV movies during this period, including *The Gambler*, which borrowed its title from Rogers' 1970s hit record. With his big beard, rugged likeability, and gravelly singing voice, Rogers was a true crossover success.

Crystal Gayle and Kenny Rogers both won Grammy Awards in 1978.

"Don't It Make My Brown Eyes Blue"

A good example of the difference between 1960s and 1970s country style happened when Loretta Lynn's younger sister, Crystal Gayle, came on the music scene. With her nearly floor-length hair, beautiful voice, and stunning good looks, Gayle was guaranteed pop success. Early on, Gayle teamed up with a songwriter named Alan Reynolds, who had success writing for both country and rock audiences.

Gayle scored big time with her dramatic signature song "Don't It Make My Brown Eyes Blue." She later joined with Eddie Rabbit on another crossover hit, the love ballad duet "You and I." These romantic love songs were a far cry from her big sister's brutally honest portrayals of the good and bad of country life.

Welcome to Hollywood

Because of country's mainstream success, several TV shows and films featuring country stars were released in the late 1970s and through the 1980s. During this time it seemed like every Nashville musician wanted a piece of the action in Hollywood, and every big star in Hollywood wanted to try on a cowboy hat.

The biggest movie hit to fuse country's rugged style with Hollywood's bright lights was 1980's *Urban Cowboy*, starring John Travolta. The movie started up a pop culture trend of its own. For a brief period, mechanical bull riding became a fad in Hollywood thanks to the movie, which was set in a honky-tonk bar called Gilley's in Pasadena, California.

As well as writing and performing its hit theme song, Dolly Parton starred in the 1980 office comedy *9 to 5*. In 1984, Parton starred opposite Sylvester Stallone in the comedy *Rhinestone*, in which she tried to turn a city boy (Stallone) into a country star.

On TV screens, *The Dukes of Hazzard* was one of the most popular shows of the early 1980s. Set in rural Georgia, it followed the misadventures of a couple of cousins and their family, as well as their stunt-driving exploits in the supercharged car they called the "General Lee." Outlaw country star Waylon Jennings provided the theme song and the off-screen commentary as "The Balladeer."

In the mid-1970s and early 1980s, the CB radio craze hit the United States. These radios are devices used by truckers to talk to one another. Because of the popularity of movies such as *Smokey & The Bandit* (which starred Burt Reynolds and Sally Fields), truckers and Southern culture were **romanticized** as sort of a modern version of American cowboy life. Country music provided the soundtrack.

Hollywood and country music met in the 1980s movie Urban Cowboy, *that starred John Travolta.*

Return to roots

Rootsy country rockers Alabama, and vocal group The Oak Ridge Boys, gave a glossy sheen to country music. But underneath was a genuine love of old-time country music. In fact, one of Alabama's first hits, "Mountain Music," was a stomping, rocking, nostalgic song about wanting someone to *"play me some mountain music like grandma and grandpa used to play."* The Charlie Daniels Band, led by fiddle whiz Daniels, bridged country rock, pop, and old-school country with their 1979 hit "The Devil Went Down to Georgia." The song combined the volume and drive of hard rock with the catchy melodies and production of great pop music. The song tells the story of a young kid who battles the devil in a fiddle duel. The old-time, "real country," and honky-tonkin' style of the kid's fiddling wins out over the devil's slick, distorted playing. This was a direct commentary on the slick pop sounds coming out of Nashville at the time.

The New Traditionalists and Young Country

In the late 1980s and early 1990s, some Nashville-based musicians started to rescue country music from the world of pop. The so-called "New Traditionalist" movement began in the late 1980s with artists including Alan Jackson, Randy Travis, and Vince Gill performing honky-tonk style country music—simple songs about everyday life. Although the records were slickly produced and had a "pop" feel, the songs were still pure country. This style became immensely popular. These artists, along with female performers like Reba McIntyre and Trisha Yearwood, filled arena-sized halls and sold millions of albums.

The artist that most helped the style's crossover to pop audiences was Garth Brooks. Brooks' brand of rock theatrics, mixed with down home country, struck exactly the right chord with fans. His 1990 album *No Fences* sold 16 million copies. It remains the biggest record sales success of any country album. His popularity led to increased sales for his contemporaries.

Around this time, a radio format known as "Young Country" began popping up on FM dials around the United States. At a time when the most popular rock music featured the loud and heavy music of grunge bands, such as Nirvana and Pearl Jam, Young Country provided an alternative for more mellow tastes.

Garth Brooks was a honky-tonk singer at heart, but with one eye on rock 'n' roll.

In the ensuing years, singers Faith Hill and Shania Twain greatly refined this middle-of-the-road style with huge pop hits that had very little in common with traditional country music. This was very similar to what happened in the late 1970s. People liked the music, but it was a far cry from country's traditional roots.

There were acts that countered this trend toward Las Vegas-style showmanship and pop songwriting. A Texas trio named the Dixie Chicks were rooted in traditional country music. A simple fiddle, guitar/banjo and vocals completed the sound.
The Chicks started their career as a traditional bluegrass band. By the late 1990s, they had developed a more pop-oriented sound that resulted in their 1998 album, *Wide Open Spaces*. The album's sales rivaled the albums of the biggest stars of the genre. Their 1999 follow-up album, *Fly*, cemented the Dixie Chicks' place among the country acts able to fill arenas.

Shania Twain performing in Nashville in 1999.

The Dixie Chicks, (from left to right) Emily Robison, Natalie Maines, and Martie Maguire.

Alternative Country

In the late 1980s and 1990s, many punk bands found inspiration from traditional country. These bands blended punk, rock 'n' roll, folk, and country. By the 1990s, this fusion of music had a couple of new names. Some called it alt.country, named after web discussion board shorthand for "alternative country." Others called it No Depression, named after the Carter Family song covered by the country-punk band Uncle Tupelo on their seminal album of the same name.

The alternative country scene respected country's roots. Uncle Tupelo drew inspiration not just from the Carter Family, but also from the early records published by Acuff-Rose. Songwriters such as Texan Alejandro Escovedo bridged the gap between country rock and folk's singer-songwriter form to create haunting portraits of loneliness, heartbreak, and love. Robbie Fulks epitomized a kind of fiery, classic, honky-tonk country music that had no place in the flashy Nashville pop system.

The individual members of Uncle Tupelo took the music even farther when they broke up. The two main songwriters, Jeff Tweedy and Jay Farrar, started the bands Wilco and Son Volt. While Farrar's Son Volt remained grounded in a hard-edged country rock style, Tweedy's Wilco quickly branched out into more experimental territory.

Meanwhile, the **multi-platinum** soundtrack to the film *O, Brother Where Art Thou*, featuring folk-country/bluegrass classics, and the *Down From the Mountain* compilation created a new market for old-time country. As recently as 2004, country music grand dame Loretta Lynn turned fans and critics' heads with *Van Lear Rose*, her Grammy-winning collaboration with rocker Jack White of the White Stripes. Lynn wrote all the songs for the album.

In its second century, country's staying power as a unique form of American music seems all but guaranteed, thanks to its rich cultural heritage and its widespread popularity among people from all walks of life.

The Uncle Tupelo sound was a mix of country-rock, country-punk, and alternative country.

Chicago-based record label Bloodshot Records became an independent success story by releasing the kind of country music that can't find a home anywhere else.

Starting in the mid-1990s with the rise of the alternative country movement, artists including Robbie Fulks, Alejandro Escovedo, punk legend Jon Langford, and country rock heartthrob Ryan Adams released critically acclaimed singles and albums for the Bloodshot. The White Stripes' Jack White also recorded for the Bloodshot label while he was still a member of the band Two-Star Tabernacle. Adams has since moved on to major label success.

Bloodshot's records have found varying degrees of popularity—some records sell only a thousand copies, while others sell hundreds of thousands. For many, the label's commitment to releasing music that celebrates country's many roots proved to be a refreshing alternative to major label pop-country music. For over a decade, Bloodshot has helped to carry the flame of old-time country to a new generation of eager listeners.

Timeline

1619 The first slave ship crosses the Middle Passage of the Atlantic Ocean.

1861–1865 American Civil War. This war between the Union and the Confederacy ended in 1865 with the defeat of the Confederates.

1865 Thirteenth Amendment to the U.S. Constitution abolishes slavery.

1877 Invention of the phonograph by Thomas Edison.

1914–1918 World War I. This war was fought between France, Britain, and the United States against Germany. Germany was defeated in 1918. The United States did not enter the war until 1917.

1920–1929 The "Roaring Twenties." This decade is also known as "The Jazz Age."

1920 Commercial radio broadcasting begins in the United States.

1922 First Country music recordings of fiddler Eck Robertson are made.

1927 Ralph Peer records the Carter Family and Jimmie Rodgers in Bristol, TN.

1929 The U.S. Stock Market crash begins the period of the 1930s known as the Great Depression.

1933 Jimmie Rodgers dies.

1939 Bill Monroe invents bluegrass with his song "Mule Skinner Blues."

1941 The United States enters World War II. The war ends in 1945.

1944 *Billboard* publishes the first "country" music chart.

Late 1940s–1973 Period of U.S. involvement in Vietnam. Involvement in Vietnam in the 1960s through 1973 is commonly called the Vietnam War.

1952 Harry Smith releases *The Anthology of American Folk Music*.

1953 Honky-tonk star Hank Williams dies at age 30.

1954 Elvis Presley records "That's All Right Mama" at Sun Studio, Memphis, TN.

1959 The first Newport Folk Festival.
Rock 'n' rollers Buddy Holly, The Big Bopper, and Richie Valens die in a plane crash over Iowa.

1963 Assassination of President John F. Kennedy on November 22nd.

1965 Bob Dylan plays electric at Newport Folk Festival.
Folk–rock band the Byrds form, Los Angeles, CA.

1968 Assassination of African-American Civil Rights leader, Martin Luther King Jr. in April.
Assassination of presidential candidate Robert F. Kennedy, brother of late President John F. Kennedy, in June.
Violence erupts in Chicago during demonstrations at the Democratic National Convention in August.

1990 Garth Brooks releases his smash hit record "No Fences."

1992 Uncle Tupelo release *March 16–20, 1992*.

2004 Loretta Lynn releases *Van Lear Rose*.

Glossary

acoustic instrument that does not have electric amplification

blacklisted to be on a list of people who are being punished, or excluded, for their opinions or actions

bluegrass style developed in the 1900s of fast-paced southern American country music, usually played on banjo and guitar

blues unique American form of folk music developed from slave culture in the United States that spread throughout the South during the 1900s

bona fide legitimate

countercultural lifestyle of people who reject the dominant values, culture and behavior of society

cover when artists record their own, newer version of another artist's music

crossover song that is popular with members of more than one set of fans (for example, country and blues)

devotional religious song about the virtues of devotion to Jesus or God in the Christian faith

Dust Bowl (era) from 1931–1939 in the American southwest-central states (especially Oklahoma), droughts, erosion, and great dust storms caused millions of farmers and others to flee west

entrepreneur someone who starts their own business

fiddle term used for a violin in country and folk music

field recorder someone who travels somewhere specifically to record an artist from that location

folklorist someone who studies and documents the folk culture of a place

G.I. person enlisted in the U.S. armed forces, especially the army

Great Depression period from 1929 until the beginning of World War II in which the United States economy was "depressed," or in poor shape," and many Americans were without work

hybrid crossover between two different genres

mandolin small stringed instrument with a pear-shaped body

medicine shows traveling shows in which salesmen would try to sell medicinal cures of dubious quality to country folk

multi-platinum album that has sold more than two million copies in the United States

nostalgic wanting to return to an earlier time or place

oral tradition folk method by which songs and stories are passed from generation to generation

punk rock a loud, fast-moving, aggressive form of rock music

race records recordings made and marketed specifically to African Americans

romanticized thinking about something in a romantic, unrealistic way

virtuosity exceptional technical skill in playing an instrument

yodeling form of singing in which the singer alternates the sound of their voice from its natural sound to an unnaturally high pitch in rapid succession

Further Information

WEBSITES

Smithsonian Music resources:

www.si.edu/resource/faq/nmah/music.htm

PLACES TO VISIT

Grand Ole' Opry

2804 Opryland Dr.

Nashville, TN 37214

615-871-6779

Country Music Hall of Fame and Museum

222 Fifth Ave. S.

Nashville, TN 37203

615-416-2092

Experience Music Project

325 5th Ave. N.

Seattle, WA 98109

877-367-5483

www.emplive.org

Huge, interactive music museum and archive.
Covers all types of popular music—jazz,
soul/R& B, rock, country, folk, and blues.

Rock and Roll Hall of Fame Museum

One Key Plaza

751 Erieside Ave.

Cleveland, OH 44114

216-781-ROCK

www.rockhall.com

Huge museum that covers rock, folk, country,
R&B, blues, and jazz.

RECORDINGS

The Carter Family:
Anchored in Love:
Their Complete Victor
Recordings
(Rounder Records)

Jimmie Rodgers:
The Essential Jimmie
Rodgers
(RCA)

Hank Williams Sr.:
Best of Hank Williams
(Mercury Nashville)

George Jones:
The Essential George
Jones: The Spirit of
Country
(Epic/Legacy)

Johnny Cash:
The Essential Johnny
Cash
(Columbia)

Willie Nelson:
The Essential Willie
Nelson
(RCA)

Patsy Cline:
The Essential
Collection
(Spectrum)

Dolly Parton:
Ultimate Dolly Parton
(BMG)

Gram Parsons:
GP/Return of the
Grievous Angel
(Almo Sounds)

Uncle Tupelo:
March 16–20, 1992
(Rockville)

Loretta Lynn:
Van Lear Rose
(Interscope Records)

Index